Front Cover: *The Women by Northumberland artist John Charlton.* Courtesy of Laing Art Gallery, Tyne and Wear Archives and Museums/Bridgeman Images.

THE NORTH EAST COAST

HISTORIC TALES FROM GRACE DARLING TO THE MAURETANIA

KEN SMITH

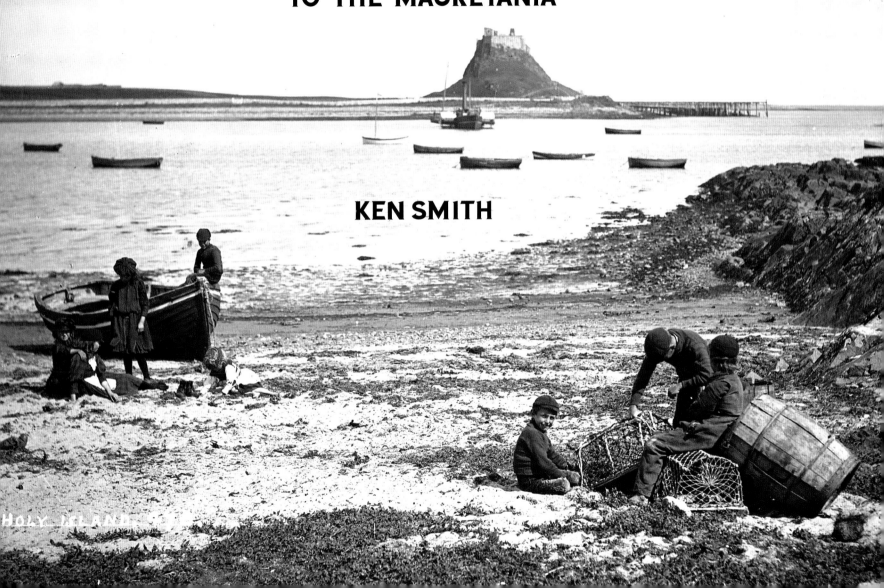

HOLY ISLAND

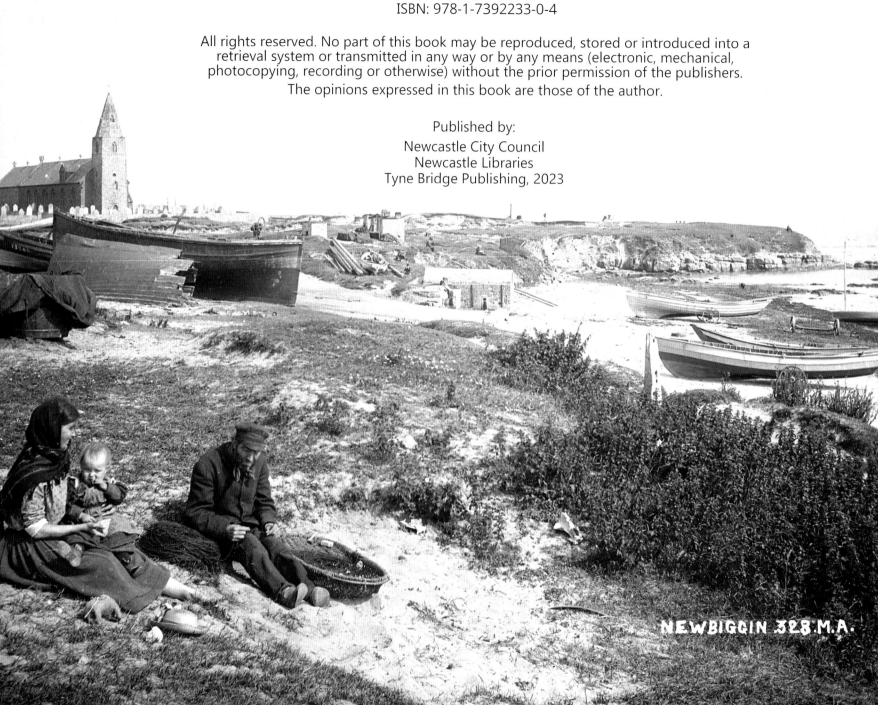

© Ken Smith

ISBN: 978-1-7392233-0-4

Published by:
Newcastle City Council
Newcastle Libraries
Tyne Bridge Publishing, 2023

NEWBIGGIN 328 M.A.

CONTENTS

GRACE AND THE FORFARSHIRE

Grace Darling was born on the Northumberland coast at Bamburgh in 1815, but except for a few brief periods on the mainland spent most of her life on two of the nearby Farne Islands.

She first lived with her family on Brownsman Island, one of the Outer Farnes, where her father, William Darling (pictured), had succeeded her grandfather, Robert, as lighthouse keeper. Later, in 1826, the family moved to Longstone, almost the outermost of the Farnes, where a new lighthouse had been completed that year.

In September 1838 the steamship *Forfarshire* was on her way from Hull to Dundee. Unfortunately, the vessel, which was carrying 41 passengers and was manned by a crew of 22, developed a leak in one of her boilers and she struggled to make progress in rough seas.

The *Forfarshire* managed to reach a position off St Abb's Head, north of Berwick, but her engines failed and she was now virtually helpless amid the storm. At least one sail was then brought into action to stop her being driven ashore.

It seems the captain then decided to try to reach the sheltered channel to the south between the Inner Farnes and the

The house in which Grace Darling was born.

Northumberland mainland. The ship was probably out of control by this time and instead of reaching the channel, known as the Inner Sound, it began moving relentlessly towards the Outer Farnes.

At 3am on September 7 1838 the *Forfarshire* struck the Big Harcar, a rocky islet, within sight of the Longstone. Eight crewmen and one passenger managed to escape from the wreck in one of the ship's boats. Then the immense seas

7

HULL & DUNDEE.

THE DUNDEE & HULL STEAM-PACKET COMPANY'S
SPLENDID AND POWERFUL STEAM-VESSEL

FORFARSHIRE,

150 *Tons Burden, and* 200 *Horse-power*

CAPTAIN JAMES MONCRIEFF,
IS APPOINTED TO SAIL AS UNDER, WEATHER, &c., PERMITTING:

FROM HULL.				FROM DUNDEE.			
WEDNESDAY,	6 December,	10	p.m.	SATURDAY,	2 December,	11	p.m.
"	13	"	5	"	"	9	"	10	"
"	20	"	9	"	"	16	"	11	"
"	27	"	4	"	"	23	"	10	"
1838.				"	30	"	11	"
WEDNESDAY	3 January	9	"	1838.			
"	10	"	4	"	SATURDAY	7 January	10	"
"	17	"	8	"	"	14	"	11	"
"	24	"	3	"	"	21	"	10	"
"	31	"	7	"	"	28	"	11	"

FARES.

MAIN CABIN £1, 5s.—FORE CABIN 15s.
DECK (Common Soldiers and Sailors), 7s. 6d.

Provisions, Wines, and Spirits, to be had on board, on very moderate terms.

Berths must be secured at the Company's Offices; and Passengers are requested to be in attendance half an hour before the advertised time of sailing.

Particulars as to Freight of Goods, Carriages, Live Stock, &c., by the FORFAR-SHIRE, which is extremely reasonable, may be had of WILLIAM JUST, Manager, Dundee; JOHN GARIE, Agent, Perth; or of

GEORGE CAMMELL,
AGENT, HULL,
1s, EAST SIDE THE HUMBER DOCK;

By whom Goods intended for Shipment, by this rapid and regular conveyance, will be *carefully dispatched,* when *specially addressed* to his care.

NOVEMBER 1837. D. ANNAS, PRINTER, DUNDEE

Poster showing Sailing Times of "Forfarshire"

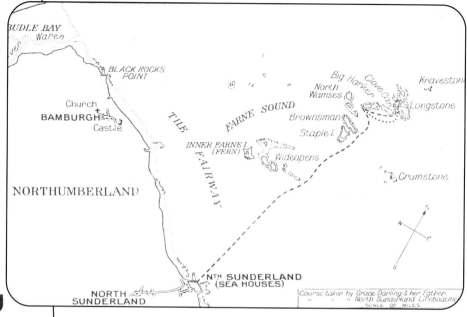

shattered the *Forfarshire*, breaking her in two. The after section, with its cabin accommodation, was swept away along with most of the passengers and crew. The captain and his wife were among those who lost their lives.

Those who survived, on the fore section of the vessel, managed to clamber on to the Big Harcar rock, holding on as best they could as the heavy seas battered the islet. Among them was a mother, Sarah Dawson, with her two children, a girl and boy. These tragic youngsters died on the rock from exposure.

In the early hours, perhaps a little before 5am, Grace Darling, then aged 22, looked out from a window of the Longstone Lighthouse and spotted what was left of the wreck on the Big Harcar. It was indistinct at that early hour, but she knew it was a ship.

At around 7am Grace and her father could make out perhaps three or four survivors on the rock. They decided to attempt a rescue despite the heavy seas. William did not believe that a rescue boat from North Sunderland (Seahouses) would be launched in such conditions.

Longstone Lighthouse at the end of the 19th Century and, inset, the building today. It was the home of Grace Darling. Modern photo: Tom Yellowley

LONGSTONE FARNE ISLAND. 475.

9

Having lived on two of the Farne Islands for nearly all her life, Grace was very familiar with the ways of the sea and was clearly skilled at rowing and manoeuvreing a boat.

Grace and William Darling set out in their rowing boat, a 21ft coble, on their errand of mercy as the heavy seas pounded the Farnes. They did not head directly for the rock, but took a more sheltered course, although this was a longer route. Eventually, they succeeded in reaching what turned out to be nine survivors, rather than the three or four they had expected.

William realised that their small boat could not take all nine, so it was decided that four men and the mother who had lost her children should be the first to be rescued. Grace used her rowing skills to look after the boat as her father gathered the survivors together to board it.

Two of the rescued men then assisted Grace's father to row back to the Longstone. It was a difficult journey against the wind and tide, while his daughter tended to the grief-stricken Sarah Dawson and a man who had been injured.

Once safely in the shelter of the lighthouse Grace and her mother, Thomasin, looked after these five survivors. William, helped by two of the men who had been saved, then made a second trip to the rock and picked up the remaining four survivors. Again, against great odds, they managed to return to the lighthouse safely.

As these events were happening, a group of fishermen had put out from Seahouses in a rescue attempt. One of the seven men in their boat was Grace's brother, William Brooks Darling.

They managed to reach the Big Harcar but only after Grace and her father had already accomplished the rescue. The fishermen found the bodies of three people on the rock,

A sketch of the wreck of the Forfarshire.

including the two children. However, the rough sea conditions made it unsafe for the boat crew to return to Seahouses and they took refuge on the Longstone.

Of the 63 people who sailed from Hull in the ill-fated *Forfarshire*, only 18 had survived. Nine lived to be accommodated for three nights in the Longstone Lighthouse. During this time it was impossible for them to reach the mainland because of the storm. The other nine survivors, who had taken to one of the ship's boats, were picked up by a sailing vessel which landed them safely at South Shields.

In an era when the idea of a young woman playing a major role in rescuing people from a shipwreck amid a storm was considered extraordinary, Grace's heroic action was greeted with high admiration and praise. Indeed, she became a national heroine and received several offers of marriage.

Queen Victoria recognised her courage and sent her a gift of £50. She was even invited to appear on stage in London. However, Grace did not let all this fame and publicity go to her head. She remained modest despite the immense acclaim she received.

Yet tragedy was to intervene to cut short this brave young woman's life. She developed tuberculosis, which during the 19th Century was a common disease. Then known as consumption, the illness was at that period incurable. Attempts to improve Grace's health by sending her for spells on the mainland at Wooler and Alnwick were unsuccessful.

The heroine of the Farne Islands died at Bamburgh in 1842, four years after the rescue, and is buried in the village's St Aidan's Churchyard within sight of the sea and across the road from the cottage in which she was born. She was aged 26.

A monument, not far from her grave, features a sculpture which depicts Grace lying peacefully, flanked by an oar. A canopy is positioned above the figure. Her grave, in which other members of her family are also interred, can be found a short distance to the south of the memorial.

The sculpture superseded an earlier one which had suffered from weathering due to sea air and wind. This earlier statue can now be seen inside the church.

St Aidan's also features a stained-glass memorial window to Grace. It depicts the three virtues of Charity, Fortitude and Hope. These were of course all qualities which Grace displayed. The window has three sections. The middle section shows Fortitude holding an oar, which many people would identify as representing Grace, although it is clearly not intended to be a likeness of her. She is flanked by Charity holding a heart and Hope an Anchor.

The Longstone Light still beams out its warning to shipping, although it is now automatic and no keeper lives on the island. Looking out today from Seahouses or Bamburgh towards the lighthouse we can remember Grace, compassionate daughter of the sea.

11

+FORTITUDE+

Clockwise from top, left, The Grace Darling Memorial, the central panel of the memorial window, St Aidan's Church and, inset, the earlier statue of Grace.

BIRTHPLACE OF THE LIFEBOAT

For centuries, the entrance to the River Tyne posed great dangers for ships and their crews. South Shields, on the southern shore of the river mouth, became the birthplace of the first all-purpose-built lifeboat, *The Original*, and the town's pilots as well as those from North Shields played a key role in the early lifeboat service when shipwreck was a frequent occurrence.

Sailing colliers and other vessels were often driven on to the stretch of coast at the river entrance by storms or gales. They might end up aground on the Herd Sand at South Shields or hit the treacherous Black Middens rocks off Tynemouth. Ships could also come to grief in the turbulent, shallow waters of the Tyne Bar, a ridge of sand and shingle stretching across the river entrance.

The Willie Wouldhave lifeboat.

In 1789, the collier *Adventure* was wrecked on the Herd Sand during a strong gale. The ship was only a few hundred yards from the beach, but the sea was so rough that Shields boatmen were unable to attempt a rescue.

Seven of the *Adventure's* crew, plus the captain, were lost. A crowd of people gathered on the beach, helpless to intervene because of that fateful few hundred yards of raging seas. Some of the unfortunate crewmen clung to the rigging but then fell into the waves.

The tragedy which befell this ship and other vessels at the river mouth led to the development of the first all-purpose-built lifeboat. The *Adventure* disaster had spurred a social group of South Shields businessmen and others – known as the "Gentlemen of Lawe House" - to start a fund and hold a competition with a prize of two guineas for the best designed rescue vessel. The result was *The Original*.

The "Gentlemen of Lawe House" set up a committee which recommended that the craft should be of considerable

A print of The Original published in 1802.

The treacherous Black Middens, c1900

Ships in difficulty always drew a crowd. Here the Fair Maid is stranded at Cullercoats in 1899.

buoyancy with an identical bow and stern so that the boat did not have to turn around in heavy seas. They indicated that the bow and stern should be high to keep out the sea as much as possible and the boat should be of shallow draught. The committee therefore stipulated the fundamental concepts. There has been much controversy over who invented this boat. Both William Wouldhave, a house painter and parish clerk of St Hild's, South Shields, and Henry Greathead (pictured), a boatbuilder of the town, put forward designs and other men also suggested ideas.

Wouldhave even built a tin model boat which featured air boxes for buoyancy and cork as a material for the same purpose. The tin model had a high canoe-like bow and stern, which were identical, and a flat bottom. His idea was that the lifeboat should be self-righting if capsized.

Greathead's craft was also flat-bottomed and did not apparently feature air boxes or cork. But the committee rejected both Wouldhave and Greathead's designs and so there was no winner of the two guinea prize.

Despite this, they offered Wouldhave one guinea – half the prize – a probable indication of their admiration for his efforts and ingenuity. They adopted Wouldhave's idea of cork, although it was certainly not a new one and the committee were likely to have been aware of the possible use of this material even before they saw his design.

In 1785, Lionel Lukin, a London-based coachbuilder, had designed a boat, which he claimed to be unsinkable, by modifying a Norwegian craft. He had added cork and air compartments to the vessel for increased buoyancy. Archdeacon John Sharp, of the Bishop Crewe Charity at Bamburgh Castle, got to hear of Lukin's design and was keen to try it out for saving lives in the sea off Northumberland.

The Archdeacon sent Lukin a Northumbrian coble (distinctive boat of the North-East coast) which he converted using his idea of cork and air compartments. This boat was thus a modification of an existing craft and not a completely new vessel like *The Original*. Whether Lukin's boat was actually used for lifesaving at Bamburgh is unclear, although Lukin believed that it was.

Nicholas Fairless and Michael Rockwood, two leading members of the South Shields committee, produced a clay model from which, they said, *The Original* was built. Although "The Gentlemen of Lawe House" took into account Wouldhave and Greathead's proposals they also assessed ideas from a number of other men. What emerged was a mixture of concepts from various sources which went towards creating the lifeboat.

One fact is beyond doubt, Henry Greathead was given the job of building *The Original*, but this was under the direction of the committee. In addition, he was to be awarded £1,200 by Parliament, which officially recognised him as the inventor, a move which only served to fuel the controversy of who was responsible for the design.

As built, *The Original* had a relatively high, pointed bow and stern, a layer of cork along the sides both inside and out for buoyancy, a clinker-built overlapping wood design, sturdy construction and, at the suggestion of Greathead, a curved keel to aid manoeuvrability.

The Original, which was oar-pulled like all early lifeboats, saved several hundred lives during a long career between 1790 and 1830. This pioneering craft carried out her first rescue on January 30, 1790, when she saved the crew of a vessel driven on to the Herd Sand, the place where the *Adventure* had met disaster the previous year.

William Wouldhave had recommended that the lifeboat should be built of copper to prevent her tearing on rocks, an idea which was rejected. It was ironic therefore that *The Original's* career was ended when the wooden-hulled craft was damaged on rocks. However, by that time she had proved her worth in many rescues.

Other pioneering lifeboats based at the mouth of the river, such as the *Northumberland* and the *Tyne*, put in sterling work too. The South Shields-based Tyne saved more than 1,000 lives between 1833 and 1877. The North Shields-based *Northumberland*, built by Greathead in 1798, also notched up an impressive rescue record.

The Shields lifeboats were manned by the Tyne pilots, who guided ships in and out of the river. They were the natural men to operate the lifeboats as they knew the local waters intimately. But the pilots, who displayed great courage, were not immune from danger. This was tragically illustrated in December 1849 when the lifeboat *Providence* capsized. Twenty of her 24-man crew were drowned. She had been on

Photo: South Tyneside Libraries

The Tyne lifeboat on display in 1890. It saved more than 1,000 lives.

her way to rescue the crew of the brig Betsy, of Littlehampton. Those who died are commemorated by a plaque in St Aidan and St Stephen's Church, on the Lawe Top at South Shields. A plaque in the church also commemorates the 19 men of the steam pilot boat Protector, who were lost when their vessel hit a mine or was torpedoed outside the river entrance during the First World War.

Today, the Tyne lifeboat is the centrepiece of The Lifeboat Memorial in Ocean Road, South Shields, which commemorates Wouldhave and Greathead. The town honours both men who endeavoured to save lives by their practical ideas.

Lifeboats Bedford, Tom Perry and Willie Woodhave in the Tyne harbour for the Pilots Conference, c1913.

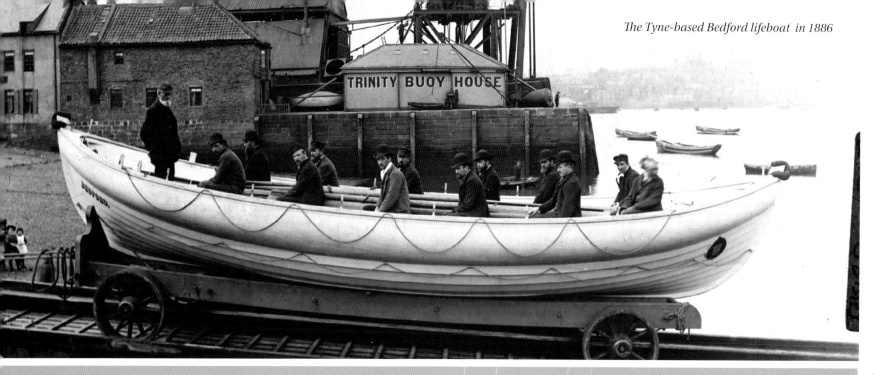

The Tyne-based Bedford lifeboat in 1886

Two of today's lifeboats in action at Cullercoats Harbour Day.

THE LOVELY NELLY

In the winter of 1860-61 the brig *Lovely Nelly*, a two-masted sailing ship, was hit by a formidable storm off the North-East coast. Amid raging seas and a blizzard she struggled to reach the safety of harbour.

The skipper of the *Lovely Nelly* may have been seeking the shelter of the Tyne but she was unable to enter the river as the heavy seas and wind moved her relentlessly away. Men of the Coastguard at Tynemouth observed that the vessel was in distress and carried shore-to-ship rocket equipment with them as they followed her northwards along the coast. The date was New Year's Day, 1861.

The stricken ship, with a crew of seven, reached a point level with the Brier Dene at Whitley Bay.

She was now virtually out of control and the skipper decided to run the ship ashore on Whitley Sands. Tragically, the vessel struck rocks or sand well off the coast. It was too far for a rocket to be fired in an attempt to get a line to the ship.

Accordingly, the Cullercoats Lifeboat was called out amid the storm of sleet and snow and was pulled by six horses the three miles to Whitley Sands at the Brier Dene. It is likely that the Cullercoats fisherwomen helped to move the lifeboat out from its house and perhaps to have assisted in pulling it to the beach at the Dene.

The Lovely Nelly, as dispicted by the Illustrated London News.

A rescue attempt from Cullercoats village was too risky in the heavy seas as it would have meant a long journey to reach the ship. It was therefore decided to try a direct approach from the sands at the Brier Dene.

The oar-pulled boat, named *Percy*, which was manned by a crew of 15, managed to reach the side of the *Lovely Nelly* and the six men aboard the ship, who had takcn to the rigging, were rescued. Three of these had been swept into the sea but luckily were pulled to safety by the lifeboatmen.

Only one member of the *Lovely Nelly's* crew was left aboard, Tommy Thompson, a cabin-boy. He was still clinging to the rigging, too frightened to move from his position. Attempts by the lifeboat crew to save him failed and he was drowned.

The loss of Tommy was one of the saddest endings imaginable to an otherwise successful rescue.

A contemporary report in the *Newcastle Daily Chronicle* (January 2, 1861) stated that as the lifeboat headed for the beach it grounded on rocks, but people watching from the shore ran into the water and pulled the vessel clear. The crew of *Percy*, all Cullercoats fishermen, were cheered by the spectators for their courageous rescue. Surviving crew members of the *Lovely Nelly* were reported to have been carried on the shoulders of spectators.

Today, in the Laing Art Gallery in Newcastle there is an impressive painting by Northumberland artist John Charlton depicting Cullercoats fisherwomen helping to pull the lifeboat to the scene of the *Lovely Nelly* rescue. The women are shown pulling the lifeboat down a snow-covered bank of the Brier Dene and on to the beach. A boy and a considerable number of men are also taking part in the effort.

Entitled *The Women*, the painting, which dates to 1910, reminds us that wives and daughters as well as husbands and sons offered support to such compassionate missions. Whether the women of the fishing village actually helped pull the lifeboat to Whitley Sands on this particular occasion is uncertain. No written record of the time seems to have mentioned this, but there is a spoken tradition that they did. It is therefore possible that the women did indeed help to pull the lifeboat, perhaps along part of the route and particularly on the descent to the beach

In addition, despite the doubts, it is likely that the Cullercoats fisherwomen sometimes helped to pull the craft out for launching and retrieve it from the sea afterwards.

John Charlton, who knew Cullercoats well and may have seen

The Women by John Charlton. Photo courtesy of Laing Art Gallery, Tyne and Wear Archives and Museums/Bridgeman Images.

the women at such times, was clearly inspired to paint this wonderful art work by their humane endeavours.

During the Second World War there were some similarities to the *Lovely Nelly* drama further north on the Northumberland coast. In February, 1940, around 30 women of Newbiggin-by-the-Sea helped to haul and push a lifeboat across land for a considerable distance in appalling weather conditions to launch the craft for a rescue. Together with a number of men, the women braved a gale and sleet as they battled over rough terrain, including sand dunes.

On this occasion the lifeboatmen, led by Second Coxswain George Taylor, managed to save the entire 11-man crew of the Belgian coaster *Eminent* which had run aground to the north of Church Point. The women of Newbiggin had in great measure contributed to saving them from the perils of the deep.

PIONEER OF STEAM

The iron-hulled, propeller-driven *John Bowes* is generally regarded as the most important pioneering steamship to carry coal from the North-East. The Tyne-built vessel certainly made a great impact when she entered service in 1852.

The *John Bowes* demonstrated that a steamship could deliver her cargo to its destination with a speed and a regularity which a sailing collier could not hope to match.

The pioneering vessel was launched at the Jarrow shipyard of Palmer Brothers on June 30, 1852. The naming ceremony was performed by the wife of Charles Palmer, the Tyneside businessman whose ideas had led to the building of the ship.

Ironically, the vessel's birth had been prompted by competition from land transport. The development of railways led to the fast delivery of coal to London and the South-East from the mines of the North Midlands and Yorkshire.

Mine owners in the North-East were worried by this challenge. There was even talk of delivering coal by rail from the Tyne to London. But Charles Palmer, who had been born at South Shields and had shares in collieries, believed the challenge from steam on land could be met by the use of steam on the sea. Charles became one of the directors of the newly-formed General Iron Screw Colliery Company, which he and other businessmen had formed to operate steamships on the coal runs from the North-East.

Pioneering steamship John Bowes.

The Newcastle Journal commented a few days after the launch of the *John Bowes* that "for 600 years have the denizens of the coaly Tyne been content to transport the black diamonds to various parts of the world in the old fashioned sailing collier, and the lapse of time has scarcely witnessed any improvement in their construction. The immense opposition given to sea transport by the establishment of railways caused Palmer Brothers & Co., to build the *John Bowes*".

Charles Palmer had founded his shipyard at Jarrow on the banks of the Tyne with his brother, George, a year earlier and the new collier was only the second vessel built there. However, within a few years the construction of steam colliers was to become one of the mainstays of the yard.

The launch of the ship stirred up a great deal of interest on Tyneside. Charles Palmer was more than happy to attract publicity for the venture. Coal owners and manufacturers were among the large number of people who attended. Guests included the Mayor and Sheriff of Newcastle. At 2.15 in the afternoon, which was high tide, the ship, nearly 150ft long, glided into the Tyne without any major problem.

Afterwards, 300 guests attended a dinner at the yard, followed by a ball in the evening. Charles and the Mayor's wife led off the dancing. Hopes for the success of the *John Bowes* must have been high.

Those hopes were to be fulfilled in great measure. The ship left the Tyne on her maiden voyage with a cargo of coal on July 27, 1852, under the command of a Captain John Scott. She halted at Sunderland for compass adjustment. From there, it took her two days to reach London, two days to discharge her cargo in the Thames and she was back in the Tyne on August 3. The round voyage had taken her only seven days, as against a sailing collier's usual month. She carried 500 tons of coal, although she was capable of taking up to 650 tons.

The Ilustrated London News recorded the launch of the John Bowes on the 30th June 1852 at the Jarrow shipyard of Palmer Brothers.

This fast voyage had been achieved even though the *John Bowes* had been "running in" her new engines by operating them at little more than half speed. Her two single-cylinder engines had been built by the renowned firm of Robert Stephenson at Forth Banks, Newcastle. This machinery gave her a top speed of about eight or nine knots. Later in the ship's career, she was fitted with new, improved engines, although like most early seagoing steamers she also carried sails, being rigged as a topsail schooner.

Palmer's yard at Jarrow went on to build many more steam colliers. It was not long before the speed and coal-carrying achievements of the *John Bowes* had been surpassed by some of these new vessels. During the year 1854 the Palmer-built steam collier *Jarrow* made 29 voyages to London, delivering a total of 18,006 tons.

In 1859, the yard built the *James Dixon*. She could carry 1,200 tons of black diamonds and made the voyage from the North-East to London and back in three days, four hours. The *James Dixon* made 57 voyages to London in one year, delivering a total of 62,842 tons of coal with a crew of 22 men. To accomplish this work with sailing colliers would have required 16 ships and 144 men.

The *John Bowes* had a long career lasting 81 years during

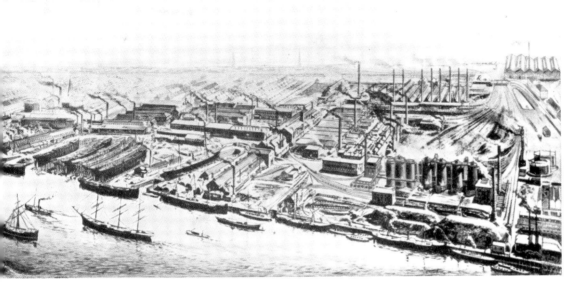

Photo: Tom Yellowley.

A statue of Charles Palmer by sculptor Albert Toft. It is today situated in Jarrow town centre.

which she carried general cargo as well as coal. In 1854 she was brought into service, along with other Palmer-built steam colliers, to carry stores and troops to the Crimean War.

However, her career had more than its fair share of accidents and mishaps. For example, on December 31, 1856, she was in collision with the *Helen Day*, of Dundee, when off Souter Point, to the north of Sunderland. The *John Bowes* received considerable damage, including the loss of one of her masts.

In 1865, the ship was involved in two more accidents. In September of that year she was in collision with a sailing vessel named the *Aimwell*, 10 miles north of Seaham. The *Aimwell* was badly damaged. December saw her run into the brig *Albion*, which was moored at North Shields. The steamer had been entering the river.

The year 1868 witnessed yet another collision. At 1am she collided with the steamer *Sappho* in the mouth of the Tyne. The *John Bowes* was inward bound at the time of the accident.

The next mishap occurred in November, 1884, at 3am. She was moving up the Thames near the West India Dock when she collided with the iron steamer *Blanche*, outward bound for Dunkirk. The *Blanche* sank, although it is not recorded whether there was any loss of life.

In September 1888, it was the turn of the *John Bowes* to receive damage. While leaving the Tyne for London her steering gear failed and she hit the South Pier, suffering serious damage to her stem. Her fore compartment filled with water. A tug took her to Jarrow Slake where she lay forlornly on the mud. However, the ship was repaired and put back in service. She was in yet another accident in December 1890, when she was in collision with the steamer *Braemar*, from Aberdeen, off Whitehill Point in the Tyne.

Photo: Parry Collection, Newcastle Libraries, W. Parry & Son, South Shields.

The Jarrow shipyard a few years before its demise as it launches the cruiser HMS York in 1928.

The John Bowes passsing Palmers yard 54 years after her launch.

The *John Bowes* was involved in a number of other mishaps and collisions over her long career, including several in the Thames. Also during her 81-year lifetime she had several changes of ownership and name.

Eventually, after a long and useful but accident-packed life, she came to grief in 1933 off the coast of northern Spain. She was sailing under the name of *Villa Selgas* for Spanish owners.

The old ship sank after developing a leak in rough seas. The vessel had been carrying a cargo of iron ore. All the crew were saved.

By a strange irony, 1933 was also the year the Palmer shipbuilding business at Jarrow collapsed, leading to mass unemployment in the town.

A derelict Palmers Shipyard in 1936.

The busy River Tyne at North Shields in 1910. In 1911 more than 20 million tons of coal and coke were shipped from the river.

COAL FROM THE TYNE

The development of steam colliers helped to generate a great increase in coal shipments from the rivers of the North-East to London, which needed plentiful and regular supplies of black diamonds to produce gas lighting for the capital's streets. In the 20th Century, the power stations of the electricity industry would also provide vital work for the colliers.

Before 1850 coal exports from the River Tyne had grown to about five and a quarter million tons a year, but between then and the early 1900s the shipments increased enormously. In 1911 more than 20 million tons of coal and coke were exported from the river to London, the South-East and other ports throughout Britain and the world. In 1913 exports again reached over 20 million tons. Although this figure fell during the First World War, shipments recovered for a while afterwards, reaching a high point of 21 million tons in 1923.

This booming seaborne trade was greatly assisted by the establishment in 1850 of the Tyne Improvement Commission which made the river one of the best ports on the East Coast. Beginning in the 1860s, the commission carried out major dredging operations which deepened the Tyne and enabled it to take larger ships as well as improving life for the smaller ones.

The treacherous bar at the mouth of the river was dredged away and the Tyne for a distance of 14 miles inland from the mouth, was widened and straightened. Islands in the waterway were dredged away. Bill Point at Walker and Whitehill Point at North Shields, protruding sections of the shore which were hazardous to navigation, were removed.

The Tyne's impressive protective North and South Piers were constructed at the river mouth. Work began on the North Pier in 1854, but it was beset with problems, being breached by storms in 1867 and again, more seriously, in 1897. The structure was therefore redesigned as a straight pier, rather than a curved one. The pier was finally completed in 1909 and opened to the public the following year. The longer South Pier was begun in 1854 and finished in 1895.

The commission also improved facilities for the loading of coal so that steamers could take on their cargoes quickly and efficiently. The Tyne gained a well deserved reputation as a port for bunkering. Ships seeking to refuel their engines could

Tyne Improvement Commission advert.

Left: Tynemouth Pier in 1898 after being breached by the sea the year before. It was replaced by the straight pier that exists today, pictured right.

speedily and cheaply replenish their bunkers at staiths (loading jetties or platforms) not far from the river mouth and so achieve a quick turn-around time at low cost.

The ships moored at the staiths were attended to by shore-based workmen known as teemers and trimmers. The teemers carried out the actual loading of vessels, operating the equipment needed for this process. The trimmers, armed with shovels, would level out the coal in the holds, helping to ensure stability and enabling the hatches to be closed by "knocking the top off" the black diamonds.

One of the earliest loading methods was the waggon drop, a system in which a coal truck was lowered from the staith on to the deck of a ship. A door was then opened in the bottom of the waggon and coal would cascade into the hold.

Alternatively, a waggon would remain on the staith, the doors in its bottom would be opened and the cargo allowed to stream down a spout (also known as a chute) into the ship. This gravity spout method eventually superseded the waggon drop, becoming the most common arrangement on the North-East coast. The early years of the 20th Century witnessed the increasing introduction of electric conveyor belts, an important advance which improved the efficiency of loading, particularly at high tides.

By 1925 there were six major coal loading points on the Tyne. They were: Tyne Dock, Dunston Staiths, and West Dunston Staiths, owned by the London and North Eastern Railway (formerly the North Eastern Railway); Northumberland Dock and Whitehill Point Staiths, owned by the Tyne Improvement Commission; and Derwenthaugh Staiths, owned by the Consett Iron Company. All were equipped with gravity spouts and electric conveyor belts. Staiths were also provided by the Tyne improvement Commission at the Albert Edward Dock, North Shields.

In addition, there were a considerable number of smaller staiths, often owned by the colliery companies, such as the Harton High and Low Staiths at South Shields, and those at Wallsend, Pelaw Main, Hebburn, Jarrow (Springwell Staiths), Felling and Elswick.

One of the most important loading facilities was at Tyne Dock on the south bank, which by 1925 had exported more coal than any other dock in the world. In 1908, 7.5 million tons of coal and coke had cascaded from its staiths into the holds of waiting ships. The dock had four staiths, which enabled 16 vessels to load at the same time. There were 42 spouts and eight electric conveyor belts. Two or more spouts could be operated on one steamer simultaneously, thus achieving rapid loading.

The London and North Eastern Railway declared in an advertisement of 1925: "Tyne Dock has the reputation for giving the quickest despatch in the country to vessels taking coal. Situated near the mouth of the River Tyne, the dock offers exceptional facilities for quick bunkering."

At Northumberland Dock, Howdon, on the north side of the river, which was opened in 1857, there were eight staiths, four operated by coal companies of south-east Northumberland and four by the London and North Eastern Railway.

Also on the north side, on a bend in the river a little to the east of Northumberland Dock, were the Whitehill Point Staiths. These were often used by bunkering ships, which did not have time to enter the dock and which could be replenished with coal at any state of the tide. However, these staiths also loaded colliers with their cargo.

The facility featured three hydraulic lifts which could raise trucks up to 45ft above the jetties, allowing large ships to be loaded with coal by electric conveyor belts no matter how high the tide.

Ten miles up river, beyond the great bridges across the Tyne between Newcastle and Gateshead, lay the important Dunston Staiths, opened in 1893. These were built to handle coal from pits west of central Newcastle and Gateshead to save the time and cost taken by the longer rail journey to the docks nearer the river mouth. A second set of staiths was added to the facility in 1903.

At Dunston, the loading of ships from the six berths could also be undertaken at any state of the tide, a tribute to the dredging work of the Tyne Improvement Commission. Each

Waggon drop system at Wallsend Staiths, illustrated by T.H.Hair.

Clockwise from top: Staiths at Pelaw Main, c1890, Tyne Dock, North Shields and South Shields.

berth had two gravity spouts and there were three conveyor belts.

Colliers steamed up river to Dunston, moving through the open Swing Bridge as crowds of walkers on the Newcastle and Gateshead sides waited patiently for them to pass. When close to the staiths they would generally moor at lines of buoys (tiers), joining a queue of vessels waiting for their turn to load.

In 1923 West Dunston Staiths were opened, over a mile to the west, expanding the facilities. Furthest west of the major coal jetties were the Derwenthaugh Staiths. These were situated a little to the east of the Scotswood Bridge on the southern bank close to the mouth of the River Derwent, a tributary of the Tyne.

The facilities at Dunston, West Dunston and Derwenthaugh, between 10 and 11 miles from the sea, had been made possible by the commission's dredging work and by the removal of Newcastle's bridge of low arches and it replacement with the Swing Bridge in 1876.

The year 1924 saw 6,007 ships pass through the Swing Bridge, the majority of them colliers. As a ship approached the bridge, from either direction, she sounded three blasts on her steam whistle. The bridge then answered this signal with three blasts on its own siren and the opening machinery was started.

In the 1930s two new staiths were opened at Howdon and Jarrow,, featuring electric conveyor belts which delivered the coal to special towers from which it was loaded on to the waiting ships. The Howdon staith, at the western end of Northumberland Dock, was opened in December 1932 by the chairman of the Tyne Improvement Commission, Harry Everett. Visiting a sub-station, he switched on the electric current, enabling coal to be loaded into the colliers *Dagenham* and *Corbrook*. The Jarrow facility began operating in 1936.

However, the mundane staiths of the Tyne were not without their moments of drama. Most were constructed of timber, making them a major fire risk.

At about 10pm on March 3, 1905, a fierce blaze broke out at Cramlington No. 5 Staith at Whitehill Point. It was believed that an axle on a coal truck had become overheated and had set fire to the truck. Whatever the cause, the flames quickly spread to the wooden staith which was saturated with tar and covered in coal dust.

The North Shields and dock fire brigades were quickly on the scene but the fire had spread rapidly and they arrived to find the 500ft-long staith engulfed in flames. The glare lit up the sky and could be seen for miles around. The firemen were unable to get within 50ft of the staith because of the intense heat.

With difficulty, an engine managed to haul a line of blazing trucks off the staith. The fire then spread to a timber shed which was burnt to the ground. At about midnight the entire staith collapsed, sending up a shower of sparks which fell on to pit props lying nearby. These too were set ablaze.

The Cape liner *Johannesburg*, which had been taking on bunker coal, was towed away from the staith on fire amidships. She was said to have been lucky to escape destruction.

The blaze was not put out until 14 hours after it began. The German steamer *Mongolia*, arriving in the Tyne early on March 4, reported that the glare of the inferno had been seen four miles off the coast.

Luckily, there had been no loss of life or injuries. Tools owned by the staith's workmen were destroyed when the timber shed in which they were stored burnt down. The Tyne Improvement Commission agreed to compensate them for their loss. Cramlington No. 5 Staith was eventually rebuilt.

Ships at Dunston Staiths in the 1920s.

Dunston Staiths in 2007.

BLACK DIAMOND PORTS

The Tyne was the most important coal port on the North-East coast, shipping more black diamonds than any other, but it was not the only one. Sunderland, Seaham Harbour, Blyth, West Hartlepool and Amble also featured prominently in the booming "sea coal" trade.

At Blyth, a staith had been opened as early as 1788 on the southern side of the River Blyth entrance. This facility was extended by the London and North Eastern Railway in the 1880s. The railway and the Cowpen Coal Company also developed their own staiths on the north side of the river, the last being the West Staiths, which began operation in 1928. At that date the port had four sets of staiths, three of them on the northern bank.

The development of Blyth as a port was greatly helped by the formation of a harbour commission in 1882 and deepening of the river which had once been notoriously shallow.

Amble, at the entrance to the River Coquet, also handled coal shipments. Staiths were developed here from the 1830s onwards at the Radcliffe and Broomhill quays, named after two nearby collieries. Also in the 19th Century, the West Hartlepool docks were opened and staiths here became important for shipping coal from pits in the south of County Durham.

Coal being loaded at Sunderland docks in the 1950s.

At Sunderland, the Hudson Dock, on the south side of the entrance to the River Wear, was opened in 1850 and extended in 1855. The Hendon Dock, adjoining the Hudson, was opened in 1868. These docks contained important staiths for loading coal from the County Durham pits, particularly those owned by the wealthy Londonderry family.

Blyth Harbour c1890. A staith with ships alongside is visible in the background.

Amble Harbour c1895.

Further up the Wear, on the south side, were the Lambton and Hetton staiths, while facing them to the north stood the Wearmouth Staiths. One of the first steam colliers to regularly load at Sunderland was the *Lady Alice Lambton*, built in 1853 and owned by the Earl of Durham. It is possible she was the first steamer to call at the Lambton Staiths (also known as Lambton Drops).

Seaham Harbour was developed in the late 1820s to handle shipments from the 3rd Marquess of Londonderry's County Durham collieries. It began operation in 1831 and was improved over the years, becoming a flourishing port. Seaham Harbour had the reputation among ship crews of being the most difficult on the North-East coast to sail into because of its narrow entrance. They nicknamed it the "hole in the wall".

Although many of the vessels leaving Seaham were bound for London and other southern ports there were also links with Hamburg. The self-discharging steam collier *Herman Sauber* was completed in 1912 by William Doxford at its Pallion shipyard, Sunderland. She had been ordered by Sauber Brothers of Hamburg for the Seaham Harbour-Hamburg trade.

A unique vessel in her day, the *Herman Sauber* had a conveyor belt system of discharging her cargo, patented by Doxford's. With two conveyors working on each side, she was able to discharge up to 1,200 tons of small coal per hour. The cargo could be unloaded in all weathers and covered delivery chutes rendered the process almost dust-free.

Busy river activity at Sunderland, c1895.

North Dock, Seaham Harbour, c1895.

Following the First World War the ship was handed over to Britain as part of Germany's reparations, coming under the management of the Pelton Steamship Company of Newcastle. But she was eventually sold back to the Sauber firm.

On October 30, 1922, the *Herman Sauber* sailed from Seaham Harbour for Hamburg with coal. By the early morning of November 3 she was encountering heavy seas and her cargo shifted, rendering her unstable. She then capsized and crewmen were thrown into the waves in the darkness.

Photo: Tyne and Wear Archives and Museums.

The second Herman Sauber. She capsized after sailing from Seaham Harbour in 1922.

All were lost, except one man who clung to an oar. When daylight came he was picked up eight miles from Spurn Head by a Grimsby trawler. Although utterly exhausted, the man revived and was taken to hospital at Grimsby. The skipper of the trawler reported seeing bodies in the water.

The Sauber Brothers' coal business with the North-East must have stretched back many years for in 1876 another of their steamers, also named the *Herman Sauber*, was described as a regular trader between the Tyne and Hamburg. This ship became the victim of severe southerly gales in December 1876.

She was on passage from Hamburg to Sunderland to load coal, but when she arrived off the mouth of the Wear her master, a Captain Vogel, considered it was too dangerous to attempt crossing the bar in heavy seas. With difficulty, he took his ship northwards to the Tyne but again he found the conditions so bad that he would not attempt entering the river.

Forced to stay at sea, the captain took his vessel as far north as the Farne Islands. The weather remained severe, the starboard lifeboat was carried away and the ship's decks were constantly swept by the rough seas.

Provisions were running low, and Captain Vogel decided to make a second attempt to enter the Wear. But yet again he was forced by the raging seas to turn his ship away. The *Herman Sauber* then headed towards the Tyne for a second time. By now it was Christmas Eve and the ship had been battling for nearly six days to make port.

As she attempted to get safely into the river she was struck by a heavy sea which put her steering gear out of action. The *Herman Sauber* was now helpless. She drifted ashore on to rocks at South Shields.

However, the ordeal of those aboard was nearly over. The famous lifeboat *Willie Wouldhave* succeeded in rescuing all her 19 crew. These were lucky men. Four days earlier the steamer *Tyne*, owned by George Otto of North Shields, had sunk near the same spot with the loss of 17 crew.

TURBINIA IN THE NORTH SEA

The Turbinia.

People looking out from the Northumberland coast in the 1890s may have seen a sleek, one-funnel boat dashing along at great speed through the waters of the North Sea. This unique craft was *Turbinia*, the world's first steam turbine-driven vessel.

Turbinia was the creation of Charles Algernon Parsons, a brilliant engineer who trained on Tyneside. He had designed this extraordinary boat to demonstrate the advantages of his invention, the marine steam turbine engine.

Parsons, one of six sons of the Third Earl of Rosse, was born in 1854 in London, but the main family home was at Birr Castle, County Offaly, Ireland. His father was a distinguished astronomer and had achieved great fame by building a large reflector telescope, measuring six feet across.

After private tuition, Charles Parsons continued his education at Trinity College, Dublin, and St John's College, Cambridge, where he achieved high honours in mathematics. There were no courses in engineering at this period.

After leaving Cambridge University in 1877 he joined the Elswick Works of W.G. Armstrong & Co., by the River Tyne in Newcastle. His position was as a so-called "premium" apprentice, a post which he paid £500 to secure. Such apprentices were not destined to become ordinary craftsmen and were more likely to rise to managerial rank or achieve

distinction with another firm. His training was followed by a post with a Leeds engineering company.

At the beginning of 1884 he became a junior partner with the ship equipment manufacturers Clarke, Chapman & Co., of Gateshead, and headed their electrical department.

Parsons now took one of the most significant steps in his career by inventing a steam turbine engine for driving a dynamo to generate electricity. With typical ingenuity and perseverance he overcame the extreme difficulties of developing this high-speed engine in which the force of steam is applied to blades on a rotor.

The engine proved a complete success. Clarke, Chapman began manufacturing these steam turbo-generators to provide electric lighting for ships. The first vessel to be lit by this new equipment was the *Earl Percy* of the Tyne Steam Shipping Company.

The turbine engine was clearly a machine of enormous potential for the electricity industry and it would not be long before Parsons' turbo-generators were supplied to power stations.

In 1889 he ended his partnership with Clarke, Chapman. Together with friends, he formed a company, C.A. Parsons & Co., which set up a works at Heaton in Newcastle, and further developed and expanded production of turbo-generators.

By late 1893, Parsons was pressing ahead with his plan to apply his invention to ships by designing *Turbinia*, the unique boat that would demonstrate to the world the advantages of using the steam turbine upon the seas. For this purpose he and a group of five associates formed a new business, the Marine Steam Turbine Company.

The firm proclaimed that the turbine engine would "enable much higher rates of speed to be attained than have hitherto been possible with the fastest vessels". It listed other assets of the turbine as including a reduction in vibration and in the space occupied by machinery aboard ship, so increasing a vessel's carrying capacity. Significantly, the company also stressed the new engine's ability to reduce the consumption of steam.

To find out what would be the most suitable design of hull for *Turbinia* and the power needed for it, Parsons made model boats and tested them out on a pond at Ryton-on-Tyne. The first model was only about 2ft long and is said to have been towed by a fishing rod and line, but later a 6ft model, driven with the aid of a twisted rubber cord, was used. Tests were also carried out on a pond at the Heaton Works.

Photo: Tyne and Wear Archives and Museums.

The Turbinia's engine room.

Turbinia was to be a sea-going greyhound and to ensure that she would not be encumbered by too much weight her hull was built of extremely thin steel. Accordingly, the task of constructing the boat was given to Brown & Hood, a sheet metal firm of Wallsend. The steel for the vessel was made in Jarrow.

The boat which took shape at Wallsend is extremely long and narrow. Designed purely for speed, she is 103ft 9ins long but has a beam of only 9ft. Her sleek appearance and knife-edge bow impress visitors to the Newcastle Discovery Museum today in much the same way as they impressed spectators in the 1890s and early 1900s.

Launched into the Tyne in August 1894, *Turbinia* then began a long series of trials off the Northumberland coast. This, however, was only possible when conditions were calm enough, but unfortunately this was frequently not the case. *Turbinia* had an extremely low freeboard (the distance between the waterline and the open deck level) and her displacement was a mere 44.5 tons. Consequently it was wise for her to avoid rough seas.

The boat moored at the Turbinia Works, Wallsend.

True to form, the enthusiastic Parsons sailed on the trials, braving with the rest of the 10-man crew the inevitable soakings which occurred at high speeds as sheets of water swept the deck and spray filled the air. Parsons was normally in charge of the controls in the engine room cab.

Turbinia's captain and lookout was Christopher Leyland, a director of the Marine Steam Turbine Company who lived at Haggerston Castle, near Beal in north Northumberland. A very wealthy man, he owned an estate of more the 20,000 acres and invested a large sum of money in the company.

Leyland was a former naval officer and a keen horticulturalist and botanist. He pioneered the cultivation of the Leylandii cypress tree, which was named after him, and planted vast numbers of trees of varying species on his estate.

The boat's helmsman or "steersman" was Robert Barnard, a manager of the company who had supervised *Turbinia's*

construction and helped with her design. His steering, guided by Leyland's ever-watchful eyes, was often vital in avoiding collisions.

Despite this alertness, there were some mishaps. On one occasion disaster could not be prevented because the reversing gear was unsatisfactory. Impeded by a current, the vessel found difficulty in making a turn while in the river and struck the side of the cargo steamer *North Tyne*. The knife-edge bow of *Turbinia* punched a hole in the ship over a foot long despite the efforts of Parsons and the rest of the crew to stave off the accident with boat hooks. The *North Tyne* required a new plate to repair the damage.

The trial runs were not always exclusively masculine affairs. Women sometimes joined men on the trials at sea and when some runs were made along the Tyne. Charles Parsons' wife, Katherine, and his daughter, Rachael, were aware that they were likely to be drenched along with the rest of the crew.

Crew members pose for a photograph alongside at Wallsend.

Charles Parsons stands by his cab from where he controlled the engines and, inset, Lady Parsons.

On one voyage off the mouth of the Tyne Captain Leyland spotted a 23-knot warship which had been built at Armstrong's Elswick Works in Newcastle. *Turbinia's* crew must have regarded the ship as an opportunity for amusement and a playful challenge. They battened down the hatches and Parsons accelerated the vessel to 28 knots.

In a short space of time *Turbinia* had overtaken the warship which gave a good-humoured blast on her siren as if to acknowledge the turbine boat's superiority of speed.

The bow wave thrown up by this display of high speed came sweeping over the deck and Katherine, Rachael and Parsons' son, Algernon, who was also aboard, were completely soaked. Wisely, the two children went below to the forward stokehold to dry off. Members of the crew did not escape the water either. Officers aboard the warship later said that all they saw

of *Turbinia* was a bow emerging from a huge wave and a flame from the funnel flickering into the air.

Another lady who sailed on the trials was Miss Leyland, the daughter of the captain. Crew members spoke of her as a "thorough sport" and she clearly enjoyed the thrill of speed at sea as much as anyone else. A soaking was perhaps part of the excitement.

Down in the boat's two stokeholds conditions were extremely cramped. In the forward stokehold there was only room for one man at a time to swing his short-handled shovel. When exhausted, the man would lean against one of the feed pumps while the next stoker took his turn at shovelling the coal. The conditions were indeed uncomfortable, but the contribution of these unsung men was vital to *Turbinia's* power.

Photos: Tyne and Wear Archives and Museums.

A stern view at over 30 knots. Inset: The liner Queen Elizabeth and the Turbinia as depicted on a Parsons' brochure.

Upon returning to the Tyne from trials, stokers were sometimes employed on other tasks as the vessel lay moored at Wallsend, her permanent base. One of these jobs was to repaint *Turbinia's* yellow funnel after each trip. Steersman Robert Barnard said of this task: "We do that after every run because the fire licks the paint off when we drive her fast with forced draught." The flame from the funnel would "wind round the smoke-stack like a scarf round your neck".

During the first half of 1897 *Turbinia* clocked up over 30 knots on her trials. The boat eventually reached a maximum speed of around 34.5 knots, equal to nearly 40 land miles per hour.

In the same year Parsons' steamed *Turbinia* south from the Tyne to Spithead, between Portsmouth and the Isle of Wight, where she staged an unofficial display of her speed at Queen Victoria's Diamond Jubilee Review of the Fleet. At this event a vast array of warships from the Royal Navy as well as visiting foreign vessels was assembled.

The inventor of the marine steam turbine could not have chosen a better stage on which to put *Turbinia* through her paces. Dashing past the lines of warships, she achieved a speed of 34.5 knots in front of the people that Parsons needed to influence. As usual, the inventor was at the controls in his engine cab and Leyland stood atop the vessel's conning tower on lookout.

This astonishing display of speed proved to be the turning point for the fortunes of the turbine engine on the sea. The breakthrough came in 1898 when the Admiralty placed an order for a torpedo-boat destroyer, *HMS Viper*, to be built by Hawthorn Leslie at Hebburn on the banks of the Tyne, with Parsons' company supplying the engines.

HMS Viper, the world's first turbine-driven warship which achieved nearly 37 knots on her trials in 1899.

Soon afterwards, the Admiralty decided to buy a second Parsons' turbine-driven ship of the same type, which was already being constructed by Armstrong Whitworth at its Elswick Yard in Newcastle. This vessel would also be named after a snake, *HMS Cobra*.

However, although the *Viper* and *Cobra* passed their speed trials off the North-East coast with flying colours, their careers were to prove all too brief.

In August, 1901, the *Viper* struck rocks off Alderney in the Channel Islands during thick fog. Her starboard propellers were shattered, rendering her helpless and she broke in two. Fortunately there was no loss of life and the crew managed to escape in the ship's boats. They succeeded in taking the flotilla signal book with them, but no other items of value were saved.

Then, only just over a month later, tragedy struck her sister ship. The *Cobra* also broke in two and sank off the Lincolnshire coast on her delivery voyage from the Tyne. Sixty-seven men lost their lives, including *Turbinia's* steersman Robert Barnard and other members of Parsons' staff who had been aboard the ship. There were 12 survivors.

Charles Parsons was devastated by the tragedy and for the remainder of his life was haunted by the untimely death of his dedicated men. Initially, he and his associates feared that this double calamity could affect the turbine programme. But these fears proved unfounded. The engines of the two ill-fated vessels were cleared of any blame.

The Admiralty went on to show its confidence in the invention when in 1902 a third turbine-driven torpedo-boat destroyer, *HMS Velox*, entered service. Then came the destroyer *HMS Eden* and the cruiser *HMS Amethyst*. In 1906, the first of a new breed of all-big-gun battleships, *HMS Dreadnought*, was launched and equipped with turbines.

However, the adoption of the engine was not confined to warships. Merchant vessels also began to feature on the growing list. The first passenger ship to be driven by turbines was the Firth of Clyde pleasure steamer *King Edward* in 1901, followed a year later by a sister vessel, the *Queen Alexandra*. Then, in 1905, the Allan Line ships *Victorian* and *Virginian* became the first passenger liners to be driven across the North Atlantic by turbines.

But perhaps the greatest success of all for Parsons came in 1907 when the Cunard liners *Mauretania* and *Lusitania* entered service between Liverpool and New York. Both were equipped with turbine machinery of such power that they were capable of service speeds of 25 or 26 knots. *Mauretania*, built on the Tyne, proved herself to be a speed queen of the first order.

Charles Parsons went on to be knighted and was also awarded the Order of Merit. He died in 1931 at the age of 77 and is buried, along with his wife, Katherine, in Kirkwhelpington Churchyard, Northumberland. He was undoubtedly one of the world's greatest engineers.

Advert referring to Cunard liners Mauretania and Lusitania which entered service in 1907. Both were equipped with turbine machinery.

The Turbina is the first exhibit you see as you enter Newcastle's Discovery Museum.

RESCUED FROM THE WAVES

The French steam trawler *Tadorne* was on her way to the fishing waters off Iceland in March 1913 when she ran into trouble off the Northumberland coast. The ship found herself enveloped in thick fog amid heavy seas.

In the early morning of March 29, the *Tadorne*, with a crew of 30, struck rocks off Howick Haven. The Coastguard officers at the fishing village of Craster, a short distance to the north, were alerted to the plight of the trawler by a farmer at Seahouses Farm, near the Haven. He had heard the shouts of the distressed crewmen.

The Coastguard men sprang into action and took rocket equipment to the scene in an attempt to get a line to the vessel, but she was too far off the coast and the very cold conditions made the task of attempting a rescue by breeches buoy impossible.

The Boulmer Lifeboat was now called out and in the face of the rough seas her crew rowed two miles northwards along the coast to the stricken trawler. Against great odds they managed to bring 25 of the *Tadorne's* crew safely to the shore, although they made two trips to the wreck as their boat could not accommodate all 25 at one time.

To make two journeys in such appalling conditions showed courage of a high order. The men from Boulmer, a fishing village to the south of Howick, had carried out a rescue in the best traditions of the lifeboat service.

However, five of the *Tadorne's* crew lost their lives, including one man who died in the lifeboat. The four others included a 16-year-old cabin boy.

Once safely on land, it was found that none of the surviving crewmen from the trawler could speak English. However, the Earl and Countess Grey, whose family home was a short distance inland at Howick Hall, sent a French maid from their household to act as interpreter. The Earl and Countess provided blankets and clothing for the rescued men who were also helped by people from the nearby coastal villages.

Today, a boiler from the *Tadorne* can still be seen in Howick Haven, a reminder of the tragic crewmen who died. The five were buried in the churchyard of St Michael and All Angels in the tree and flower-clad grounds of Howick Hall. Their grave is situated close to a wall of the small church and features a beautiful cross positioned facing upwards.

The remains of the Tadorne's boiler at Howick Haven.

An inscription reads: "This cross is placed here by the people of Howick, Boulmer and Craster in memory of five French sailors who out of a crew of 30 were drowned in the wreck of the French steam trawler Tadorne off the rocks at Howick Boat House on March 29 1913."

The coxswain of the Boulmer Lifeboat, William Stephenson, received a gold medal from the French government and a silver medal from the RNL for his key role in the rescue.

The *Tadorne* had been powered by steam, but over the centuries a vast number of sailing ships, many of them colliers, were wrecked off the North-East coast during storms or gales. In an era before the use of steam at sea, these vessels were vulnerable to adverse winds and were often driven on to the rocks or sand.

Just one example of how ships relying on sail power could come to grief is provided by the fierce storm of early April

The grave of the Tadorne's five crewmen at St Michael and All Angels.

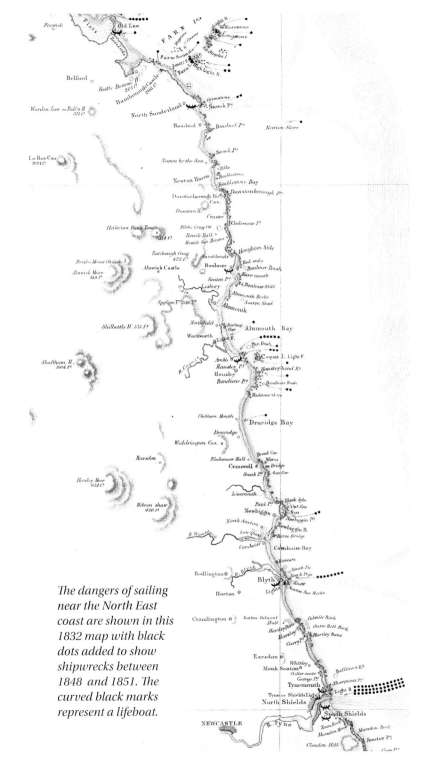

The dangers of sailing near the North East coast are shown in this 1832 map with black dots added to show shipwrecks between 1848 and 1851. The curved black marks represent a lifeboat.

1788. Within the three days before the tempest struck over 200 vessels had departed from Shields and Sunderland, most of which had to face the full power of the wind and sea. Soon reports were coming in of ships being driven ashore, often with fatal consequences.

Among the ships wrecked in this way were the *Elizabeth*, of North Shields, which was lost near Whitburn with all hands, and the *Auspicious*, and another vessel from Sunderland, which were wrecked off Newbiggin on the Northumberland coast with several crew members reported drowned.

As well as the *Auspicious*, no less than 12 other ships were said to have been wrecked between Blyth and Holy Island. They included the *John*, of South Shields, one crewman saved; the *George and Mary*, of Sunderland, lost on Cresswell Sands with all hands except the captain; the *Active*, of Sunderland, all hands lost; the *Joseph and Mary*, of Newcastle, several crewmen drowned; the *Thetis*, of North Shields, crew lost; the *Charming Harriet*, of South Shields, five saved, six drowned; and the *Elizabeth and Margaret*, of North Shields, six crewmen drowned. Luckily, all the crew of the *Gemini*, of Blyth, were saved.

Late January 1802 witnessed another storm of great power. As the wind rose three ships coming into Shields Harbour were driven on to the Herd Sand, but the tide was flowing very high and they cut their anchor cables and managed to get out to sea again. However, the *Thomas and Alice*, a brig from Blyth, was also blown on to the sand. The *Northumberland* lifeboat was launched and her courageous oarsmen pulled through the huge breakers, reached the vessel and saved the entire crew.

In 1803 the collier *Bee*, of North Shields, left her home port with a cargo of coal but was driven back by a strong south-easterly gale. The *Bee* was then swept on to the rocks of the Spanish Battery at the mouth of the Tyne. The

49

Northumberland lifeboat was launched, manned by a crew of South Shields pilots, who managed to manoeuvre their craft with great skill among the rocks and huge waves. The *Bee's* crew of six, including the master who was injured, were all rescued.

A major storm accompanied by snow occurred in late January 1815. The brig *Success* was struck by a tremendous sea as she came towards the Tyne, her masts were broken away and she was driven on to the Herd Sand. The crew, except the helmsman, were swept into the water. Six men were saved by The *Original* lifeboat. The master, mate and a boy were all drowned.

This storm raged on into the following day and the brig *Mercury,* of Blyth, struck the Black Middens rocks as heavy waves and surf continued to pound the coast. Again, The *Original* lifeboat went into action and saved the entire crew. The lifeboat suffered damage as she was dashed against the rocks.

These shipping casualties are just a small sample of the countless number which occurred over hundreds of years in the waters of the North-East coast. But although the accident record of sailing ships, many of them small, was appalling, the era of steam vessels also saw its share of casualties as the case of the trawler *Tadorne* illustrates.

One of the most tragic shipwrecks occurred in July 1843 when the paddle steamer *Pegasus* sank with the loss of 51 lives after she struck the Goldstone Rock on the north side of the Farne Islands. The *Pegasus* had been on course from Leith to Hull when she encountered disaster during the night.

After the ship hit the rock an attempt was made to run the vessel ashore on the Northumberland coast, but the *Pegasus* sank before this could be achieved. There were only six survivors, four crewmen and two passengers. Women and children were among those lost.

Another tragedy occurred in November 1864 when the passenger steamer *Stanley*, on course from Aberdeen to London, sought refuge in the Tyne during a storm. However, the vessel met disaster when she hit the Black Middens rocks at the mouth of the river. A schooner, the *Friendship*, which had already sought shelter, also ended up on this notorious reef.

Attempts by the few Coastguard men available to rescue the passengers and crew on the steamer by means of rocket and breeches buoy met with only limited success. It seems the Coastguards had to be assisted by onlookers. Three men were saved in this way, but problems with the lines plus a rising tide which put the ship out of reach of the rocket equipment meant others aboard the *Stanley* were still in great danger. Two people from the ship were reported to have lost their lives by falling into the sea during the breeches buoy operation.

An attempt to launch a lifeboat from the wrecked steamship was unsuccessful because of a collapsed davit. Five people, a man and four women, drowned as a result.

Meanwhile, the self-righting Tynemouth lifeboat *Constance* was launched and its crew rowed from Prior's Haven through the heavy seas to the bows of the Stanley. It looked at this point as though a line might be secured between the two vessels. However, the lifeboat was overwhelmed when an immense sea struck as she came close to the steamer.

Afterwards, the *Constance* collided with the schooner *Friendship*. Four of the lifeboatmen were swept into the water and ended up aboard the stricken *Friendship*. The *Constance*, which had become partly tangled in the rigging of the schooner, eventually floated off. The lifeboat crew had lost most of their oars.

Further disaster now hit the *Stanley*. Crewmen and passengers on the deck house and bridge were swept into the sea and drowned. The *Stanley* eventually broke in two and all passengers and crew on the aft section were lost. Those on the fore section of the ship were rescued the following morning by means of rocket and breeches buoy.

A total of 26 people aboard the *Stanley* lost their lives. The six crew of the *Friendship* and two of the four lifeboatmen on the schooner also perished.

This terrible double accident resulted in the formation of the Tynemouth Volunteer Life Brigade, the first such brigade in the country. The aim was to recruit a team of volunteers highly trained in the use of rocket and breeches buoy equipment who would keep a close watch on the coast and carry out rescues from the shore. Not long after its formation, volunteer life brigades were set up at Cullercoats and South Shields. In 1877, a brigade was founded in Sunderland.

The 20th Century was also to witness its share of shipping accidents along the North-East coast. One example was the coaster *Efos*, which in November 1927 encountered a strong gale and ran aground at the mouth of the Wear in Sunderland. The *Efos* was reported to have hit one of the piers. Sunderland Volunteer Life Brigade rescued the 17-man crew by breeches buoy. The ship was later towed clear by tugs and refloated.

Another successful rescue operation took place in January 1963 when the cargo steamer *Adelfotis II* ran into trouble during a furious gale. The captain decided to seek shelter in the Tyne. Her steering gear had failed and she was driven aground on the Herd Sand at South Shields. The wind blew the ship along the sand until she was next to the Groyne.

In a combined operation, the South Shields and Sunderland volunteer life brigades saved the 23 men of the *Adelfotis II*, including the captain. It is believed to have been the last

rescue by breeches buoy to take place on the North-East coast.

The First and Second World Wars had brought their own special and terrible dangers to shipping in coastal waters. German mines and torpedo attacks posed an ever present threat.

In the autumn of 1914 the Tynemouth motor lifeboat *Henry Vernon* journeyed southwards through the night in a strong gale to rescue survivors from the wreck of the hospital ship *Rohilla*, which had struck a reef at Saltwick Nab, near Whitby.

Because of wartime precautions the lighthouses along the East Coast were not illuminated and shore lights were also unlit. The *Rohilla*, which had been on her way from the Firth of Forth to Dunkirk to pick up wounded soldiers, became lost in the darkness amid the heavy seas and came to grief on the rocks. The crew of the *Henry Vernon* successfully rescued 50 people from the stricken ship after pouring oil on the sea to reduce the action of the waves. This Tynemouth motor lifeboat had shown her worth in appalling conditions. Much earlier, the crew of a lifeboat from Whitby, in the face of great difficulties, had rescued 35 others from the Rohilla. Further attempts by several other lifeboats to take off more people from the ship had failed. Over 80 lives were lost.

Another shock was to come less than two months later. On the morning of December 16, 1914, major German warships steamed through a gap in an extensive minefield to raid towns on the East Coast. They bombarded Scarborough, Whitby and Hartlepool with their powerful guns.

At Hartlepool, the bombardment led to the deaths of more than 100 people in the town. Fatalities also occurred at Scarborough and Whitby, but Hartlepool suffered the worst death toll. Numerous people were also injured. Soldiers manning a shore battery on the Headland at Hartlepool

In January 1963 the cargo steamer Adelfotis II ran into trouble during a furious gale. She was driven aground on the Herd Sand at South Shields. In a combined operation, the South Shields and Sunderland volunteer life brigades saved the 23 men of the ship, including the captain.
Photo courtesy of Shields Gazette.

Shields steam pilot cutter Protector was hit by an explosion off the mouth of the Tyne

Photo: South Tyneside Libraries.

returned fire. The warships escaped back across the North Sea via the gap in the minefield which the Germans themselves had laid on a previous occasion.

Also during the First World War, 19 men aboard the Shields steam pilot cutter *Protector* lost their lives when the vessel was hit by an explosion off the mouth of the Tyne. The tragedy, which happened on New Year's Eve, 1916, is believed to have been caused by a mine or torpedo attack. Those lost were 10 Tyne pilots, four assistant pilots and five crew. A memorial plaque to the 19 men of the *Protector* can be found in St Aidan and St Stephen's Church on the Lawe Top, South Shields.

The Second World War also witnessed extreme dangers near the mouth of the Tyne. The entrance to the river was almost blocked after the tanker *British Officer* hit a German mine in early December 1940. She had been on a voyage to the river in ballast from Sheerness when disaster struck. The tanker hit the mine a short distance outside the piers and was taken in tow by tugs.

However, the *British Officer* then grounded by the stern next to the inside of the South Pier. After a number of days she broke in two and a tug pulled the bow section away. This section was later scrapped. Most of the aft section was also eventually cleared. Five lives were reported to have been lost. The *British Officer* had been completed by Palmers of Jarrow in 1922.

The tanker was not to be the only victim of a German mine near the entrance to the river. The Norwegian passenger liner *Oslofjord* also came to grief, less than 24 hours after the *British*

Tynemouth Motor Lifeboat Henry Vernon and crew who saved 50 survivors of the hospital ship Rohilla in November 1914.

Officer's demise. The liner had been due to enter the Tyne shortly after the tanker.

The Oslofjord was built for the Norwegian America Line, which suffered heavy losses of its vessels during the war. With a gross registered tonnage of 18,673, she could carry 860 passengers and was 587ft long. This made her one of the largest ships to be wrecked on the North-East coast.

The two-funnel liner entered transatlantic service in 1938, but in 1940 she was laid up at New York and requisitioned as a troopship by the British. While on a voyage from Liverpool to Newcastle to be fully fitted out for trooping, she struck a mine laid by a German aircraft, not far from the mouth of the river. The same aircraft may also have laid the mine encountered by the *British Officer*.

One crew member of the *Oslofjord* lost his life, but the others survived, many being rescued by the Tynemouth and Cullercoats lifeboats. The stricken ship was taken in tow and beached to the south of the river entrance.

The wreck now lies south of the pier at South Shields. The *Oslofjord* suffered an additional indignity when in 1943 a cargo vessel, the *Eugenia Chandris*, hit the wreck and sank on top of her. It was a sad fate for such a fine liner.

TYNE TO TITANIC

On the morning of April 15 1912 the Tyne-built passenger liner *Carpathia* rescued the bitterly cold and traumatised survivors of the *Titanic* disaster. She had been 58 miles away from the sinking ship when she picked up her distress call and immediately responded by steaming into the night at full speed towards the *Titanic's* last reported position.

Carpathia braved numerous icebergs in the hope of reaching the stricken ship before she slipped beneath the surface of the North Atlantic. However, when she arrived at the disaster scene there was no sign of the great White Star liner which many had thought unsinkable. The *Titanic* had disappeared into the depths well over an hour previously with the loss of more than 1,500 lives.

But *Carpathia* picked up the 706 *Titanic* passengers and crew who had managed to board the ship's lifeboats. To the survivors the Tyne ship must have seemed like a miracle as she steamed out of the dawn.

Carpathia's birth on the Tyne had been accompanied, like most births, by emotions of pride and happiness. It was on April 24 1903 that the passenger cargo liner departed her fitting out quay at the Wallsend Shipyard of C.S. Swan and Hunter Ltd, which was soon to merge with Wigham Richardson's company at the Neptune Yard in Low Walker. Proud yard workers who had built her stood on the quay and cheered loudly as she began moving slowly down the Tyne for preliminary trials in the North Sea and delivery to her owners, Cunard, in Liverpool.

The Tyne-built passenger liner Carpathia.

Photo: Tyne and Wear Archives and Museums.

Photo: Tyne and Wear Archives and Museums.

The Carpathia at sea. She served on the New York-Trieste, Liverpool-New York and Liverpool-Boston routes. At the time she picked up the Titanic's distress call she was on her way to the Mediterranean, bound for Gibraltar and ultimately Trieste. The rescue ship was 58 miles to the south-east of the sinking liner.

It was a thrilling moment for them to see the finished result of their labours and craftsmenship – she was yet another ship proving to the world the high standards achieved by the Tyne's naval architects and workmen.

Carpathia's keel had been laid down at Wallsend on September 10 1901 and she was launched just under a year later, on August 6, 1902. During the early stages of building the liner, excavations in the yard had uncovered the eastern end of Hadrian's Wall, the so-called "Branch Wall" leading down towards the river's edge from the Segedunum Roman fort.

The 558ft-long vessel, bearing one tall funnel painted in Cunard's red and black livery, was 13,555 gross tons, making her one of the company's intermediate-sized liners. She was equipped with two quadruple expansion engines built by the Wallsend Slipway and Engineering Company, whose works were situated only a short distance down river from the shipyard. The engines were linked to two propellers which gave her a top speed of around 15 knots.

Carpathia was not a sumptuous luxury liner – she was built to carry second and third-class passengers. But the ship provided, for relatively cheap fares, a superior standard of accommodation for such travellers.

At the date of her completion she could take over 200 passengers in second class and more than 1,500 in third. Nearly 500 third-class (steerage) passengers were provided with cabins, including two, four and six-berth. However, the majority in steerage were accommodated in dormitory areas. Besides passengers, the liner was equipped to carry chilled beef from the United States in refrigerated compartments. Among the most important items she also carried were the mails to and from America, earning her the title Royal Mail Ship or Steamer (RMS) *Carpathia*.

After several successful trial runs over the measured mile in the North Sea, during which *Carpathia* exceeded the guaranteed speed, the ship prepared for her delivery voyage under the command of Captain Barr. After departing the Tyne, she steamed northwards around Scotland to reach Liverpool. Carpathia sailed on her maiden voyage from Liverpool bound for Boston on May 5, 1903.

It was in 1912 that Carpathia achieved world-wide fame. At this time she was serving on the Trieste-New York route, carrying mainly Hungarian and Italian emigrants to a new life in the United States. On her return trips from New York to Trieste she would also take comfortably-off US citizens on pleasure trips to the Mediterranean.

Captain Arthur Rostron, then master of *Carpathia*, could not have been aware when his ship departed New York on April 11, 1912, that he would soon be called upon to launch a humanitarian mission of epic proportions.

Rostron, who was born in Bolton, Lancashire, had been an officer with Cunard since 1895 and was given command of *Carpathia* in January 1912 at the age of 42.

As his ship cleared New York harbour early on the afternoon of April 11, another vessel on the other side of the Atlantic was departing from her anchorage off Queenstown (Cobh) in Ireland while on her maiden voyage from Southampton to New York, a voyage she would never complete.

This 46,300-ton liner, the largest in the world at that date, was a four-funnel White Star Line giant carrying more than 2,200 passengers and crew. She bore a name destined to echo down the many years which have elapsed since. That one word – *Titanic* – remains indelibly printed on the face of 20th Century history. Her maiden voyage was taking place amid a blaze of publicity with some people claiming she was virtually unsinkable. Like many ships at that time she did not carry enough lifeboats to accommodate all those aboard.

By the night of April 14 *Carpathia* was well on course for Gibraltar and about 1,000 miles east of New York. The weather had turned bitterly cold but the sky was wonderfully clear with many stars and lights of the Aurora Borealis visible.

The ship's young wireless operator, Harold Cottam, had been on duty since early morning. By just after midnight Cottam was extremely tired and he began preparing to turn into bed for the night. However, the enthusiastic young operator kept his earphones on as he began unlacing his boots.

Cottam called the *Titanic* to tell them there was a batch of messages on the airwaves for the ship. It was then that *Titanic's* radio operator butted in with an extraordinary message. He asked Carpathia to "come at once" and added: "We have struck an iceberg". The operator gave *Titanic's* position as Latitude 41.46 North, Longitude 50.14 West. He confirmed to Cottam they required immediate assistance.

The Titanic at Southampton at the beginning of her maiden voyage.

An artist's impression of Titanic in the throes of disaster from the Illustrated London News.

Carpathia's stunned radio man raced to the bridge and told the officer on the watch that *Titanic* had sent out a distress call. They then went to Rostron's cabin. The captain, who was trying to get some sleep, was irritated by their sudden entrance.

For a few seconds, Rostron found the news that *Titanic* had hit a berg and was sinking difficult to believe. Could such a disaster really be happening to this great ship on her maiden voyage? He asked Cottam if he was absolutely certain the message was correct. The operator was adamant. *Titanic* had sent out the old distress call, CQD, and the new one, SOS.

The captain's doubts were ended. He went to the chart room where he worked out that the stricken liner's reported position was 58 miles to the north-west of *Carpathia*. Rostron sprang into immediate action. He ordered the ship to be turned around. *Carpathia* began moving on a north-westerly bearing as she worked up to full steam. She was now sailing in the opposite direction to Gibraltar, towards an icefield, dotted with bergs and growlers (smaller blocks of ice).

Rostron showed efficiency and humanity as he meticulously prepared his ship for her rescue mission. He instructed that every member of the crew be served coffee to fortify them for the difficulties and hard work ahead.

The lifeboats were swung out in readiness to pick up survivors and canvas ash bags were brought out so that small children could be brought aboard in them if necessary. Boson's chairs were also made ready to lift other survivors. Gangway doors were opened and lines prepared for throwing to *Titanic's* lifeboats. Ladders were fastened to *Carpathia's* sides and strong lights sited at gangways.

Rostron told the stewards to have blankets, soup, tea, coffee and brandy ready. The two dining saloons became first aid stations and the ship's three doctors (British, Hungarian and Italian) were posted to them.

Captain Rostron was clearly determined that *Carpathia* would be in a high state of readiness by the time she reached the disaster area. But could he reach the *Titanic* before she sank? The question must have plagued him continually as his ship raced through the early hours on a glass-like sea.

The captain did what he could to ensure the vessel's engines achieved their maximum potential. Her hot water was shut off so that all available heat could be turned into steam and extra stokers were employed keeping the furnaces fed with coal. It is likely *Carpathia* achieved a speed of between 15 and 16 knots during the next few hours. Later, it would be claimed she reached 17 knots or more, but this would not have been possible for her engines. However, it is beyond doubt that her Wallsend-built engines served her well.

Whatever her speed, Rostron must have been acutely aware of the risks ahead as he began the dash to the north-west in search of the ill-fated Titanic. His ship was carrying more than 700 passengers and she was sailing at full steam during the night into waters where an icefield had been reported. It was a dangerous situation and great care had to be taken with the helm. The lives of *Carpathia's* passengers and crew as well as *Titanic's* survivors were at stake.

Accordingly, extra seamen were posted to keep lookout and it was not long before the need for such action was confirmed. *Carpathia* began encountering a series of bergs and altered course to avoid them. A sharp lookout by the crew proved effective and on at least one occasion a berg was spotted by star-shine reflected from its surface. *Carpathia* was, of course, a more easily manoeuvred ship than the much larger *Titanic* and was travelling at a slower speed.

Meanwhile, Cottam had radioed to *Titanic* that *Carpathia* was coming to their rescue as fast as she could. At 2.40am a green flare was sighted from the bridge. It was a long way ahead but it sent a signal to *Carpathia* that human life was still active in the area of *Titanic's* last reported position. In reply, at 3am

Carpathia began firing rockets at 15-minute intervals. They would tell of the rescue ship's approach, giving hope to any survivors.

The ship continued to weave her way through the icefield, with the eyes of lookouts strained towards the horizon. But as they approached the disaster area there was no sign of *Titanic*, though more green flares were sighted. Rostron must have known then that he was too late.

By 3.30am *Carpathia* found herself in the midst of countless bergs and growlers (smaller blocks of ice). Rostron ordered the engines to be put on half speed ahead. They had taken around three-and-a-half hours to get there.

Suddenly, a green flare shone out. It was almost at sea level. Then, as the first light of dawn streamed across the waters, Rostron and his men could just make out a lifeboat being rowed with difficulty towards *Carpathia*. All its occupants were exhausted, cold and numbed by their ordeal. The boat contained 25 women, ten children and five men. Four of the men were at the oars. At the tiller was a young ship's officer.

As the boat reached *Carpathia's* side, an officer and two seamen descended rope ladders and boarded her. She was then manoeuvred towards and open doorway and made fast with lines. The women and children were lifted aboard safely in bosun's chairs and canvas ash bags. The five men managed to climb the ladder to the doorway.

As the light grew, Rostron was able to make out other lifeboats scattered over a wide area. There were 20 in all, including four collapsibles.

The young *Titanic* officer in the first boat, James Boxhall, was taken to the bridge where he told Rostron that the *Titanic* had sunk. The great liner had foundered at 2.20am on April 15, 1912, with the loss of over 1,500 lives. It must have been difficult for Rostron and his crew to take in.

Women passengers sewing and distributiong clothes to help Titanic survivors aboard the Carpathia. Many had evacuated the sinking liner wearing only light clothing, or had spent some time in the water. From the Illustrated London News.

The water in *Carpathia's* vicinity was 33F, a mere one degree above freezing point. Anyone in the sea would not have survived long. *Carpathia's* crew continued the task of picking up the survivors. Her own passengers crowded the deck rails, watching the proceedings in stunned silence. Strangely, some of the boats were half empty, but others were packed to capacity.

A great number of women survivors were now widows. They searched in vain for their husbands aboard the rescue ship. Children were also without fathers. Out of eleven honeymoon couples on *Titanic*, only one man survived. One woman had become separated from her baby during the evacuation of *Titanic* but, unknown to her, the child has been taken safely aboard *Carpathia* and happily Rostron was able to reunite mother and infant.

The last of the lifeboats to reach *Carpathia's* side was carrying 75 people. It was very low in the water and in danger of being swamped or capsized. The sea was becoming choppy. However, all were embarked safely. The final person to board was *Titanic's* Second Officer, Charles Lightoller, who had taken command of the lifeboat and whose seamanship was invaluable in keeping it afloat.

In all there were just 706 survivors, although some accounts suggest there may have been five or six more. The figure may therefore have been 711 or 712. Three men died of shock and exposure soon after they were taken aboard.

An estimated total of 1,503 people had lost their lives in an ocean tragedy which shocked the world. Captain Edward Smith honourably went down with his ship. All of the liner's engineers also perished, a fate they shared with the ship's band, who, it is well attested, kept on playing until the very end.

The North East of England, where *Carpathia* had started her life, did not escape the losses. Among the crew members who died was Alfred King, described by the *Newcastle Journal* as "a promising youth of Nile Street, Gateshead". He had worked for ship equipment manufacturers Clarke Chapman of Gateshead, but had always wanted to go to sea. Alfred had been employed as a lift boy in first class. Engineer C.F.W. Sidgwick, from Sunderland, was also lost. He was on his way to a new job in Mexico and his wife had been due to follow him at a later date. They were newly married.

William T. Stead, a famous campaigning journalist and former editor of the *Northern Echo* at Darlington, was another person on the casualty list. He had been born in Northumberland in 1849.

The career of Captain Arthur Rostron never looked back after the momentous rescue of the *Titanic* survivors, who were landed safely in New York. A plaque bearing his portrait was put on show in New York's Hall of Fame and he was presented with a US Congressional Medal of Honour. Later, he was to receive the Freedom of the City of New York. Other honours followed, including the Gold Medal of the New York Life Saving Benevolent Association and the Insignia of the French Legion of Honour.

Carpathia Captain Arthur Rostron with the silver cup presented to him by Titanic survivors.

Between 1915 and 1926 Rostron commanded *Mauretania*, the Tyne's most famous passenger liner. In 1928 he was knighted, later becoming Commodore of the Cunard Line. Like the rockets he fired from his ship, he had shot to fame in one night of decisive action to save lives, but unlike the lights from those rockets his fame never faded. The compassionate and efficient captain died in 1940.

And what became of *Carpathia*? It was a German U-boat which eventually ended her career, ironically sending her to rest on the Atlantic seabed like the *Titanic*.

Carpathia was steaming in convoy from Liverpool to New York on July 17, 1918. The ships were about 120 miles south west of the Fastnet Rock, southern Ireland. It was 9.15am. Two torpedoes hit the engine room amidships and another struck the vessel's forward section. Three trimmers and two firemen were killed by the first torpedo explosion.

The ship slipped beneath the waves two-and-a-half hours later. The 275 survivors were picked up by the minesweeping sloop *HMS Snowdrop* which landed them safely at Liverpool.

The life of *Carpathia* had ended with a wartime attack, a fate she shared with many other merchant vessels of the First World War. But the liner from the Tyne and her crew had won a lasting place in the honours list of humane deeds by ships and men.

Carpathia stewards, stewardesses, kitchen staff and other crew members pose for a picture in the aftermath of the rescue.

THE SUPREME SHIP

The great passenger liner *Mauretania* was the pride of the River Tyne. Built by Swan Hunter and Wigham Richardson she was a ship of exceptional quality and outstanding performance. The vessel was the largest and most magnificent passenger ship launched on the river. She served as a transatlantic passenger liner, troopship, hospital ship and cruise liner during a glittering career lasting 28 years.

Above all, the liner was a speed queen, holding the Blue Riband for the fastest crossing of the North Atlantic longer than any other liner in the first half of the 20th Century. She frequently travelled at speeds of around 25 or 26 knots.

Mauretania was launched at Swan's Wallsend Shipyard on September 20, 1906, by the Dowager Duchess of Roxburghe. The event was watched by thousands of spectators on both sides of the river.

Christening the ship *Mauretania*, the name for the ancient Roman province of north west Africa, the Dowager Duchess broke a bottle of wine over the liner's bows. As the ship began to move towards the Tyne, steamers sounded their sirens, adding to the cheers of the crowds. She entered the water only forty seconds after starting her journey. The *Mauretania* was born.

Left: The construction of the Mauretania and, above, her launch.

There was only one accident reported during the launch. A workman was slightly injured when a piece of glass from the shattered wine bottle fell on his head. However, he was quickly given first aid and was said to be little worse for his experience.

Afterwards, the vessel was towed by tugs to her fitting-out quay and over the next year she was provided with her lavish woodwork cabins and public rooms, engines and four funnels. The huge turbine engines and boilers were lifted into the ship by the floating crane Titan.

On September 17, 1907, as *Mauretania* neared completion, she was taken down the Tyne to the North Sea for preliminary trials which lasted five days. Large crowds flocked to the river's banks to see the liner put to sea for the first time.

During her test runs the ship's speed performance was encouraging. She achieved a maximum of 27.5 knots and averaged over 26 knots while steaming between St Abb's Head in Berwickshire and Flamborough Head, Yorkshire. Carrier pigeons were released from the ship to take news of the progress of the trials to the Wallsend Shipyard. On September 21 the vessel returned to the Tyne.

A month later all was ready. *Mauretania* left the Tyne on her delivery voyage on October 22, 1907. Tens of thousands of people crowded the river's banks all the way from Wallsend to Tynemouth and South Shields, cheering the magnificent ship as she passed gracefully on her way to sea with an escort

CROWD WATCHING THE LAUNCH OF THE S.S. MAURETANIA. SEPT. 20. 1906. BALLAST HILL HEBBURN. G.H.N|C .5251.

of tugs. The liner was also saluted by the buzzers of shipyards and engine works and the sirens of ocean-going vessels and small craft.

The 31,938 gross tons *Mauretania* was 790ft long overall with a maximum beam of 88ft. She was driven by powerful turbine engines, built by the Wallsend Slipway and Engineering Company. The engines were constructed to the designs of the company's manager Andrew Laing and his team, based on

the turbine principles developed by the brilliant Tyneside-based inventor Charles Parsons and under licence from the Parsons' company. The engines were linked to four huge propellers. The liner featured four impressive funnels painted in the traditional Cunard red and black colours.

Mauretania departed on her maiden voyage from Liverpool to New York on November 16, 1907, but a storm prevented her from capturing the coveted Blue Riband for the westward

The Mauretania was 790ft long overall with a maximum beam of 88ft. She was driven by powerful turbine engines, built by the Wallsend Slipway and Engineering Company. She is pictured during fitting out at the Wallsend Yard.

The Mauretania's colours were changed during her war service. She is dressed in camouflage dazzle paint.

passage. However, on her return voyage to Britain she broke the eastward record with a speed of 23.69 knots and held on to this honour for the next 22 years.

In May, 1908, the liner broke the westward record, at last capturing the Riband for both directions. In doing so, she had beaten her Clyde-built sister, *Lusitania*. A friendly duel developed between the two vessels and in July of the same year *Lusitania* regained the westward honour. But finally, in September, 1909, *Mauretania* again achieved a record speed westwards, holding on to this accolade for 20 years. On this famous 1909 crossing she achieved an average speed of 26.06 knots. She was now the supreme ship of the North Atlantic.

Her four propellers had each been fitted with four blades, instead of the initial three, and this had improved her rate of knots.

The liner from the Tyne again achieved an average 26.06 knots westwards in September 1910, but her fastest passage was in 1929 when she notched up an average of 27.22 knots eastwards.

During the First World War, the Tyne's most famous passenger ship carried troops and also served as a floating hospital. The liner carried many Canadian soldiers to Europe. In the summer of 1915 she made three voyages to the Aegean Sea, taking troops to the ill-fated Gallipoli campaign. Later that year she was converted into a hospital ship and returned to the Aegean three more times, on these occasions transporting men wounded at Gallipoli or who had fallen sick during the campaign home to Britain. During this role as a hospital ship her hull was painted white and displayed red crosses.

The Mauretania's first class dining room.

Photo: Tyne and Wear Archives and Museums.

In 1918, *Mauretania* was again used as a troopship and temporarily renamed *HMS Tuber Rose*. She carried thousands of American soldiers from New York to Liverpool on their way to join the Allied armies on the Western Front. After the war, the liner carried many of those who had survived the conflict back to the United States. The American troops nicknamed her "The Maury".

With her trooping service completed, the ship returned to civilian duties with Cunard. Her home port was switched from Liverpool to Southampton, although her destination in North America remained New York.

In 1921, she steamed back to Swan's Wallsend Yard where she was converted from a coal to an oil-burning ship. Her oil conversion improved her performance. For the next eight years the ship successfully plied the Southampton-New York route and became affectionately known as the "Grand Old Lady of the Atlantic." The legendary ship did not lose the Blue Riband until 1929, when she was beaten by the more powerfully-engined German liner *Bremen*.

During her final years, *Mauretania* was used extensively as a cruise ship, sailing mostly to the West Indies. Her hull was again painted white. Some nicknamed her the "White Queen."

In 1931 the liner undertook three popular weekend cruises from New York to Nassau in the Bahamas. These voyages were dubbed the "Booze Cruises" because many Americans aboard were taking the opportunity to escape the Prohibition. Similar trips were also made to Halifax in Canada. In 1933 and 1934 she undertook numerous cruises to the West Indies.

At last, in 1935, she sailed for the breaker's yard at Rosyth on the Firth of Forth. But on her way northwards she stopped at the mouth of the Tyne as a tribute to her North-East origins.

The Mauretania leaving the Tyne for her preliminary trials in September 1907.

Thousands of people lined every vantage point along the seafronts at Whitley Bay, Tynemouth and South Shields and they were rewarded with a sight never to be forgotten. The liner came to a halt two miles off the piers at the entrance to the Tyne and fired rockets from her bridge as a further mark of admiration for the workmanship of the Tyne.

Small boats crowded with sightseers went out to greet her. They sounded their sirens in tribute to the great liner. The flotilla of craft was augmented by fishing vessels, tugs and the Shields pilot boat. It was a sad, but heart-warming occasion.

Flying from *Mauretania's* foremast was a 20ft-long blue ribbon, representing the Blue Riband of the Atlantic. Proudly it bore the message: "1907 to 1929."

The Lord Mayor of Newcastle, Councillor R.S. Dalgliesh, was at the North Shields ferry landing preparing to journey out to *Mauretania* when he received the following wireless telegraph message from her: "Thank you for your greeting.

For 28 years I have striven to be a credit to you, and now my day is done. Though I pass on, may Tyneside ever reach out to further and greater triumphs. With pride and affection I greet you. Farewell – Mauretania."

The Lord Mayor and his party were then taken out to the ship by the tug *Plover*. The Mayor of South Shields, Councillor J.W. Watson, also made the journey, but in a separate boat. The councillors boarded the liner and chatted for several minutes to her last commander, Captain A.T. Brown, on the bridge. Then it was time to leave. The Lord Mayor re-boarded the tug Plover and the party sang Auld Lang Syne as they stood in the tug. Others in the small craft around them joined in the singing and then people aboard the liner also began to sing.

Soon *Mauretania* was steaming slowly away from the Tyne on the final leg of her final voyage. Boats again sounded their sirens in salute and onlookers waved handkerchiefs until she was out of sight to the north. She was gone.

St Mary's Lighthouse, Whitley Bay. Photo: Newcastle Libraries

Acknowledgements

The author gratefully acknowledges the important contribution made to this book by his friend, the late Newcastle shipping historian and author Dick Keys. Dick, an enthusiastic and highly knowledgeable maritime researcher, was co-author with Ken Smith of several books, including Black Diamonds by Sea, Steamers at the Staiths, Down Elswick Slipways, From Walker to the World, and Armstrong's River Empire. Always helpful and willing to give generously of his time and knowledge, Dick, a former seaman, was an expert on sailing ships as well as steam-driven vessels.

Many thanks are extended to the author's friend, photographer Dr Tom Yellowley for his extensive picture research and for generously contributing his photographs, to retired journalist Ian Wilson for his kind help with Second World War shipping research, to Vanessa Histon and Stephen Smith for their proof reading work and last, but by no means least, to Derek Tree, manager, Tyne Bridge Publishing.

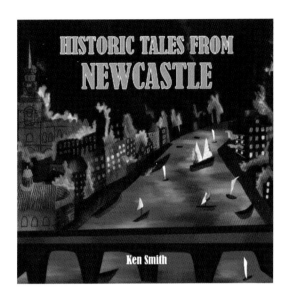

By the same author

Newcastle's colourful and sometimes dramatic history is brought to life in this series of tales spanning several hundred years. Including some of the most fascinating accounts of true stories from the city's stirring past. From the Great Fire of 1854 to explosions on the Town Moor, this book covers the major events that helped shape the city. Featuring some of it most influential figures like Lord Armstrong and George Stephenson, as well some much-loved landmarks like the Newcastle Keep and City Walls, *Historical Tales from Newcastle* is a must-read for those wanting a starting point into the history of the city.

£8.99 from
Tyne Bridge Publishing